Stop The Judgment

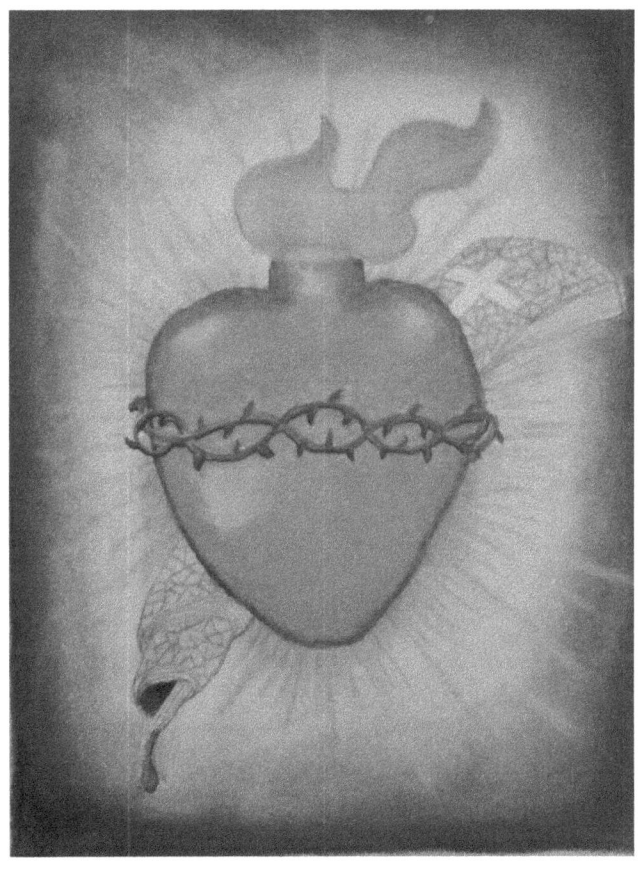

Going After the Heart of Traditional Church Folk on

Sexuality and Marriage Equality

By
Samuel Marcus Brown,
Lifetime Member of the Christian Church

Copyright © 2015 Samuel Marcus Brown
All rights reserved.

ISBN: 098603519X
ISBN 13: 9780986035197

Editing

ED Editing

&

Daniel Shack

Table of Contents

Acknowledgements xi

Introduction xiii

Preface xvii

Chapter 1
So What's the Big Fuss All About? 1

Chapter 2
Denial 5

Chapter 3
Here is The Burden 9

Chapter 4
Stop The Madness! 15

Chapter 5
"If you are a Practicing Homosexual, You Can't be a Christian" 19

Chapter 6
Who Told You That You Were Naked? 23

Chapter 7
Holy Rollers 25

Chapter 8
Why Me?   29

Chapter 9
Deliverance, Truth or Choice   33

Chapter 10
Authenticity   37

Chapter 11
Context is the Key   41

Chapter 12
And Such Were Some Of You: 45

Chapter 13
Marriage Equality is Honorable for All People   49

Chapter 14
Was Jesus Aware of Gay Folk?   55

Chapter 15
What are Eunuchs?   57

Chapter 16
Church Culture Can Be a Breeding Ground for Hypocrisy   59

Chapter 17
My Contention and Observation on
HIV/AIDS in Our Communities of Color   63

Chapter 18
Jesus is Not Your Scapegoat for Bigotry   67

Chapter 19
Evelyn & Dennis Schave, Evidence of an Olive Branch   69

Chapter 20
Reconciliation   73

Chapter 21
Uganda! Uganda! Uganda!   75

Chapter 22
More Evidence of an Olive Branch   77

Chapter 23
Thank You President Obama!   79

Chapter 24
My Conclusion   81

Epilogue   83

Works Cited   85

Dedication

I dedicate this book to my loving parents, Richard and Parthenia.

Pops, I have always taken pride in your passion as a very profound teacher of the Bible. You've always taught us that scriptural context is the key to understanding the "word of God." You have served in the capacity of a national evangelist, bishop, pastor, and associate elder over the last 50 or more years with a deep concern for the souls of God's people. I have always been impressed with your position of standing strongly for the truth and for what you believe.

Mom, I am always humbled by your selfless way of life as a local missionary. I can only hope your warm heart of helping the less fortunate, even when you have very little for yourself, has rubbed off on me. I would like to think that I am influenced by your passionate faith in prayer. I have learned that your knack for speaking the truth of your heart without reservation is respected and embraced by most in the long run.

I love you both with all of my heart and I count myself truly blessed to have come from two of the most solid people that I have ever known.

This book is also dedicated to all parents concerned about the spirituality and sexuality of their children.

Acknowledgements

I believe words such as genuine, trustworthy, non-judgmental, and supportive are great attributes for any individual. If you embody any of these characteristics, other people can testify about your character. I have been very fortunate to have people in my life who possess at least one, some, or all of these characteristics. Some are listeners, some I listen to, some are counselors, some seek counsel, some are comical, and some I make laugh. We can tell each other when we're wrong or right. I thank you for being such a special person in my life Phoebe Wallace, Charles Turk, Jerry McCoy, Calpatrick Robertson, Christina Cloman, Maxey Bennett, Steffin McNeil, Danny Norman, James Muller, Karen Lyles, William Todd, Thelma Phillips, Kisha Sims, Sean Varnado, Grant Solomon, Dwayne Wilson, Frederick Chapman, Wayne McNeil, Wayne Knox, Paul Rogers, Cherren Scruggs, Terry Richardson, Andrea Mason, Wendy Johnson, Bryant Johnson, and James Davis.

Derek Matthews, you are the one who really encouraged and pushed me to write and publish this book. You have a beautiful soul.

Mike Johnson, thank you for your friendship, feedback, and suggestions; they are very much appreciated.

Derrick Tinsley Sr. you embody each of these characteristics and I especially & sincerely thank you for being there.

> "Prejudice is a burden that confuses the past, threatens the future, and renders the present inaccessible."
> – *Maya Angelou*

Introduction

I thank you for your full attention while reading what the Holy Spirit has placed in my heart.

I am thoroughly convinced that homosexuality is not a sin. Acts 17 references the Jewish people of Berea who were considered a nobler people. They received what they were being taught in the synagogue with all readiness of mind; however, they searched the scriptures daily to determine if they were being taught the truth. This is the very reason why I have written this book. I implore my Christian brothers and sisters to examine the Bible and the verses traditionally used to condemn same gender loving, gay or homosexual people. It is so very crucial for ministers of the gospel to apply scripture within its proper context and to so-called "rightly divide the word of God" on this subject matter.

I understand you can easily dismiss the subject matter of this title as something contrary to the Christian Faith. However, your thoughts would be far from the truth. As a believer of the Bible and a follower of Jesus the Christ; I believe the word of God and the spirit of his love that establishes truth, and not religious traditions. It is my prayer that my words will enlighten and unify my Christian brothers and sisters in the faith.

In addition, my most earnest request to God is that those who have lost their faith in God and in Christian people for various reasons will be healed and restored. It is my intent to help build a bridge of love, truth and understanding between two opposing worlds of religious tradition and God's sovereignty.

I prefer you refer to the King James Bible when you analyze my opinions. It is one of the original English translation versions of the Bible, which was completed in 1611.

It is known to be historically reliable, tried and true among those in the Christian faith.

Bible scholars, as well as casual readers, have read that adding to or taking away from verses of scripture is forbidden, according to verses in the King James Bible. This version of the Bible is lauded by most preachers of the Gospel. The Old Testament was mostly written in ancient Hebrew and the New Testament was written in the common Greek language.

I read the history of newer English versions of the Bible in order to understand the need for additional English translations. After I observed some added words and changes in specific verses of scripture, I believe the main reason for the many other modern published versions since the 1940s, which were produced by various religious organizations, is to sway readers and preachers of the Bible. I am of the opinion these publishers want to subject readers to their way of thinking or ideology and their particular biased understanding of certain words, verses, and subject matter that may appear to be unclear to the average reader's understanding of "The King's English."

For instance, The New International Version (NIV) project was started after a meeting in 1965 at Trinity Christian College in Palos Heights, Illinois, of the Christian Reformed Church, National Association of Evangelicals, and a group of international scholars. The New York Bible Society, which is not biblical, was selected to do the translation. The New Testament version of the (NIV) was released in 1973 and the full Bible in 1978. It underwent a minor revision in 1984. A planned 1997 edition was discontinued over inclusive language.

The translation is a balance between word-for-word and thought-for-thought.

I ask, "Whose thought?"

> God is a Spirit: and they that worship him must
> worship him in spirit and in truth.
>
> *(John 14:17)*

> Even the Spirit of truth; whom the world cannot receive,
> because it seeth him not, neither knoweth him: but ye know
> him; for he dwelleth with you, and shall be in you.
> *(John 4:24)*

> Wisdom is the principal thing; therefore get wisdom:
> and with all thy getting get understanding.
> *(Proverbs 4:7)*

"The sovereignty of God is the biblical teaching that all things are under God's rule and control, and that nothing happens without His direction or permission. God works not just some things but all things according to the counsel of His own will. (Eph. 1:11) His purposes are all-inclusive and never thwarted (Isa. 46:11); nothing takes Him by surprise. The sovereignty of God is not merely that God has the power and right to govern all things, but that He does so, always and without exception. In other words, God is not merely sovereign de jure in principle, but sovereign de facto in practice." (Theopedia, 2014)

All of the preaching and teachings of goodness, love, peace, truth, holiness, and community are undermined when you isolate and deny another community of God's sovereignty.

God's word is the same yesterday, today, and a million years from now. However, our country's history displays the misguided and prejudiced mindset of Christian leaders who have assigned their thought process and interpretation of scripture as coming from the mind of God; however, they have totally missed the mark and have misrepresented the God of all creation.

The Institution of U.S. slavery and the Jim Crow South are perfect examples of how professed Christians mishandled and misinterpreted scripture from the Bible outside of its original context to justify colonial slavery and White supremacy in and outside of the Ku Klux Klan. Many of the Grand Wizards of the KKK were ministers of the gospel who used numerous verses in the Bible concerning slaves and slave ownership to support their stance. Should we follow the guidelines of the following verses of scripture in Exodus 21:1 or do we understand it within its proper historical context?

History does have a tendency to repeat itself.

> "Now these are the judgments which you shall set before them: 2 if you buy a Hebrew servant, he shall serve six years; and in the seventh he shall go out free and pay nothing. 3 If he comes in by himself, he shall go out by himself; if he comes in married, then his wife shall go out with him. 4 If his master has given him a wife, and she has borne him sons or daughters, the wife and her children shall be her master's, and he shall go out by himself.
>
> *Exodus 21:1*

> Marriage is honourable in ALL, and the bed undefiled:
> but whoremongers and adulterers God will judge.
> *Hebrews 13:4 KJV*

Preface

I want to stir your righteous minds. I often reflect back to my childhood hometown pastor in Harrisburg, PA, Bishop B. J. Ravenel. He always started each sermon with these words, "I have come to stir your pure minds."

I have written this book to challenge my Christian brothers and sisters of the faith and to provoke those in the ministry of Christian leadership to re-study the King James Version Holy Bible verses that are used as a tradition to condemn gay people, homosexuality and same gender love.

Also, I challenge you to re-think the tradition of the anti-homosexual doctrine that dominates the mindset of millions in the faith. I know the title of this book and the quoting of the above verse of scripture will infuriate many in and outside of the traditional religious church world.

one

So What's the Big Fuss All About?

A heterosexual is defined as somebody who is sexually attracted to members of the opposite sex, which is better known and defined by most people in our society as "straight."

A homosexual is defined as somebody who is sexually attracted to members of his or her own sex, which has been defined by society with several other terms such as gay, lesbian, same gender loving and a few derogatory terms.

Christian magazines, radio, newspaper editorials, books, websites, blog sites, social media, gospel song lyrics, and Christian TV around the world have documented an evil agenda being orchestrated by the gay, lesbian, same-gender loving, and homosexual community (recently identified by the term LGBT). Various musical artists have made it a practice to throw in condemning lines of anti-homosexual rhetoric in their narrations and ad-libs in their ministry of music.

Many Christians express that the so-called "gay agenda" dominates the news headlines, attacks the Christian faith, and the institution of marriage. Many Christians feel it has already taken over Hollywood with a negative connotation based on your belief system.

One of the latest stories that caused a media firestorm in December of 2013 is when the patriarch of a popular traditional family reality TV show, *Duck Dynasty* shared his opinion in a magazine interview of his opposition toward homosexuality among other topics based on his Christian faith and the Bible. A typical American polarizing argument and debate arose when his employer A&E suspended him for his anti-gay remarks. They quickly lifted his suspension after an uprising of his supporters inundated the TV network and the media with throngs of support. The antiquated argument and debate is that homosexuality has been defined as sinful according to their understanding of the Bible for most Christians. Gay or same gender loving people are insulted that their civil, religious, and human rights are being trampled by so-called "cherry picking Bible thumpers." They are frankly offended that the Bible has been used so divisively to demonize an entire population of God's creation.

We, as an entire society, have made great strides concerning marriage equality, the lifting of the military gay ban, The Employment Non-Discrimination Act, and human rights. There are strong organizations like the Human Rights Campaign, the National Black Justice Coalition, and countless organizations that fight every day for equality for a misunderstood people.

Some might say what else in heaven's name do those gay people want? All of the progress is wonderful for individuals who love, understand, and embrace their authenticity and for those who are allies and advocates for this minority.

Unfortunately, millions of Christians and non-Christians around the world decry same sex diversity and tolerance as something untoward to God that assaults their religion and their religious rights. This mindset produces religious intolerance which brings about passive aggression and personal judgmental behaviors from the Christian individuals who are opposed to homosexuality, which directly affects the psyche of the strong or the timid gay person as they are maligned in and outside of our places of worship.

An Atlanta Christian radio program aired a discussion around the *Duck Dynasty* controversy. Listeners were posed with this question: "Why does the sin of homosexuality raise such a heated debate in the media anytime that particular subject matter arises? Anti-gay Christian listeners were pretty much in unison. Their reactions were similar to one listener who said, "Their sin is no better than anybody else's sin. People try to make the sin of being gay worse than other sins. All sin is sin." One caller went on to explain that gay people are blinded by their sin and that they want everybody to accept their sin since they think that God made them that way, but their sin is not acceptable in God's sight. I tried feverishly for over an hour to reach that radio host to share my perspective, but to no avail.

Tradition is defined as an inherited, and established, and/or a customary pattern of thought, action, or behavior as can be related to a religious practice or social custom.

Most Christian churches have standard anti-gay rules and anti-homosexual guidelines.

Religious tradition is defined as the laws, regulations, beliefs, doctrines and practices that are handed down from one generation to another. Religious traditions can be either helpful and good or just bad. If they are in accordance with Bible scripture, they should be good and helpful. If they are contrary to the written, revealed word of God, they are just bad. Anti-homosexual tradition is upheld in the Christian church based on prejudiced, misunderstood, and mishandled scripture.

It seems fundamentally unsound for the world's largest religion that represents the gospel of Jesus Christ to be the world's police to go after and denigrate the gentle essence of an individual's sexuality with one brushstroke of the condemning color of sin. Christianity should be about love, compassion, listening, and gaining understanding in order to symbolize the adoration we have for God, the creator of all mankind. It should not be the passionate tirade against homosexuality that it has now become.

> The number one source of knowledge for the Ku Klux Klan is the Holy Bible. Members of the Klan believe in the literal truth of the Bible. One KKK member once wrote, "The Klansman pins his faith to the Bible as the revealed will of GOD." In fact many active Klansmen were ordained ministers.
> -*Michael Fisher*

two

Denial

Most traditional Christians will dare anyone not to embrace their ideology concerning the loving and intimate covenant shared in the Bible between David and Jonathan. We are trained that their relationship was nothing more than a deep brotherly love just as I love my three biological brothers.

Traditional Christians and non-Christians will accuse me or anyone else of twisting the scriptures; even if we actually read and understand the story within the context of how it was actually written.

It would be considered a so-called "holy offense" to most Christians for anyone to assume or even allow the thought of anything close to homosexuality to enter their mind as it relates to the story of David and Jonathan, which is chronicled in the Books of 1 Samuel and 2 Samuel.

Ideology is a meaningful belief system. It is a set of beliefs, values, and opinions that shapes the way a person or a group, such as a social class, thinks, acts, and understands.

Our Christian tradition and ideology has trained us to ignore the heavily passionate expressions of love shared between David and Jonathan. The King James Bible version of their story makes it abundantly clear they had a special love for each other that was expressed like no other covenant of love between two individuals throughout the entire Bible.

I have extracted nine passages of scripture from the story of David and Jonathan from 1 Samuel and 2nd Samuel. After reading the passages, I encourage you to review the story in its entirety – 1 Samuel 13 to 2 Samuel 1. Your interpretation of the story may differ from mine; however, your understanding of the story within its context is the key - not one's ideology.

> 1 Samuel 18:1 And it came to pass, when he had made an end of speaking unto Saul, that the soul of Jonathan was knit with the soul of David, and Jonathan loved him as his own soul.
> 3 Then Jonathan and David made a covenant, because he loved him as his own soul.
> 4And Jonathan stripped himself of the robe that was upon him, and gave it to David, and his garments, even to his sword, and to his bow, and to his girdle.
> 1 Samuel 20:4 Then said Jonathan unto David, Whatsoever thy soul desireth, I will even do it for thee.
> 17And Jonathan caused David to swear again, because he loved him: for he loved him as he loved his own soul.
> **30Then Saul's anger was kindled against Jonathan, and he said unto him, Thou son of the perverse rebellious woman, do not I know that thou hast chosen the son of Jesse to thine own confusion, and unto the confusion of thy mother's nakedness?**
> 41And as soon as the lad was gone, David arose out of a place toward the south, and fell on his face to the ground, and bowed himself three times: and they kissed one another, and wept one with another, until David exceeded.
> 1 Samuel 23:17 And he said unto him, Fear not: for the hand of Saul my father shall not find thee; and thou shalt be king over Israel, and I shall be next unto thee; and that also Saul my father knoweth.
> 2 Samuel 1:26 I am distressed for thee, my brother Jonathan: very pleasant hast thou been unto me: thy love to me was wonderful, passing the love of women.

Prejudice is a preformed opinion, usually an unfavorable one, based on insufficient knowledge, irrational feelings, or inaccurate stereotypes.

I want the non-believer to know and understand that believing and following the example of Jesus the Christ from the King James Bible is simple, peaceful, and comfort for your soul. I know this to be true.

We should not always adhere to the customs and traditions of man's religious doctrine. They are not always just or expedient. Leaders and members of some religious organizations impose their rules and regulations as ordained by God, which sometimes lead some people down a road of control and manipulation. Their traditional religious requirements oftentimes misrepresent the agape love of our Creator and the simplistic path of his grace through himself manifested as the Son of God, who is Jesus the Christ.

History scholars and archaeologists have proven through centuries of work that Jesus the Christ existed and that he walked this earth as a man. He was crucified for the sins of the world and he was resurrected and indeed ascended back to heaven. A believer's belief system is based on having the faith to believe and trust in Jesus the Christ for what he did for the world.

A Christian's only necessary requirement is to follow the example and instructions of Jesus the Christ for living daily in a Christ-like manner. If we follow his example, we will then have crystal clear clarity of determining what is required and what is necessary to have an authentic and intimate relationship with God.

We buy into rules and regulations of the church and the religious culture of what is suitable and what is considered sinful or forbidden in order to fit into their religious organizations. They judge others by using the order of God and the abominations of what they say he hates. It can be very damaging to the psyche of an individual born and raised in this religious culture who does not fit into the status quo of a young man meets young lady, possibly having a crush and dating their childhood sweetheart of the opposite sex with hopes of marrying that person one day.

Many of these people are battered by their family, religious leaders, and their peers with slanted scripture. They are under constant pressure that their romantic and erotic emotions for the same gender are unnatural and unequivocally not of God and certainly not the best choice for their life.

They bear the constant disdain and the expressions of contemptuous disapproval epitomizing the disparaging feelings and the emotions of condemnation. Their family, friends, and religious cohorts appear to be united together, driving home the point they are somehow foul and have made poor choices concerning their authenticity.

Those being condemned might ask themselves, "Why and how could something like this ever happen?" They become exhausted and burdened trying to make sense of the mystery of sexuality, based on religious church rhetoric.

> "If 1 Samuel 18:1-4 were about Jonathan's first encounter with a woman, theologians everywhere would be writing about this as one of the greatest love stories of all time. The story of Jonathan and his love would be the source of dozens of Hollywood films. But because the object of Jonathan's affection is a man, our cultural prejudice kicks in and we insist, notwithstanding the biblical evidence, that this could not have been more than deep friendship."
> *WouldJesusDiscriminate.com*

> "It is illogical to read homosexuality into the story of David and Jonathan because neither Jewish nor early Christian tradition ever endorses sex outside the bounds of heterosexual marriage. If you read the Bible from Genesis to Revelation, you will never see a depiction of a gay relationship, ever. Nor will you see homosexuality affirmed. You cannot get around the fact that the Bible says gay sex is flat-out wrong."
> *J. Lee Grady*

three

Here is The Burden

I was blessed, raised in a Christian home with parents who were teachers of the Bible, which is known as the "Word of God." They instilled the golden rule and imparted a conscience of moral and spiritual guidance. We were taught to study and understand the Bible within the context and the spirit of the written scripture. I am motivated to share my thoughts on this subject based on what they taught me.

In Acts 17 of the Bible, the Jewish people of Berea were considered a nobler people because they received their teaching with all readiness of mind. However, they searched the scriptures daily to determine if they were being taught the truth. I wrote this book for that same reason. I implore my Christian brothers and sisters to review the Bible and the verses that are used to condemn same gender loving people. It is so very crucial for ministers of the gospel to apply scripture within its proper context and to rightly divide the word of God on this subject matter.

Christians are taught to believe the King James Bible is what establishes the truth of who we are in most all aspects of Christian life. The tradition of assailing gay people in the name of God as a religious rite derives from nothing but personal prejudice and fear. Christians who participate in that kind of ungodly and unloving behavior are certainly not basing it on scripture, nor do they properly represent the Conservative Christian right.

I do not believe it is logical to go along with a church tradition that undermines God's sovereignty. We should interpret the Bible historically correct and in the spirit of love for our Creator and love for our brothers and sisters. Study means to learn about a subject by reading and researching. Moreover, an interpretation establishes and explains the meaning and significance of something. History explains the past events of a period in time or in the life or development of a people, an institution, or place.

When we use the Bible to make a specific point, we should refer to a particular verse within its context and the spirit of the matter at hand. Context describes the circumstances or events that form the environment within which something exists or takes place.

In the Old Testament, Jesus was predicted to revolutionize the world through his life, death, burial, and resurrection. He did not come to abolish Law of Moses. He fulfilled it by shedding his blood and becoming the sacrificial lamb for all of our sins. He is known today as the "Lamb of God."

Jesus Christ's life was created by God to create environments of love, sacrifice and repentance. He fed the poor and healed those with physical and mental maladies. He imparted the importance of understanding the purpose of his life to his disciples and the people of the era when he existed on earth. He empowered them to proclaim his truth. Jesus challenged the religious leaders and their traditions of the day that required everyone to obey the Law of Moses. They performed rituals, ceremonies, and traditions, including the sacrificial blood of goats, oxen, sheep, and bullocks to cover the sins of mankind along with many other religious rituals and traditions of men posturing in the tabernacles and synagogues.

Religious leaders resented Jesus for his new teachings about the power of faith, love and repentance, which after his death now covers sin.

At that time, they frowned upon Jesus healing people on the 7th day of the week, which went against their religious traditions of keeping the Sabbath Day holy. They hated Jesus who called them out on their hypocrisy for the things they did and allowed on the 7th day of the week along with all of their other inconsistencies.

When Jesus left the Earth and was resurrected back to heaven, he left us with a gift called the Spirit of Truth, better known as the Holy Spirit or the Holy Ghost – a comforter and conscience of our souls.

Churchgoers have a tendency to complicate, categorize, and place each other in hierarchal systems. People tend to rank a person's religious worth based on his or her education, socio-economic status, sexuality, and profession. When we apply such systems to environments, such as spiritual and Kingdom of God, we minimize and compromise the gifts that flow from the Holy Spirit within individuals. However, if we challenge these hierarchies, we can make the world a better place.

The church world and the concept of being a "Christian" have been polluted by unloving customs and the judgmental traditions of religion. Those who seek love and truth find their pathway shrouded by these traditions that dim the radiant light of love they so desperately seek from real Christian people. These spirit and truth killers continue to hold themselves and some of God's children in bondage. They give Christianity a bad name instead of walking in the truth and spirit of the New Covenant that was established through the sacrifice of Jesus the Christ.

Jesus is the reason and the meaning of why Christianity exists. I am amazed how the bodies of believers who are followers of Jesus read scripture within context and then misinterpret specific verses so badly to condemn homosexuality or same gender loving people. We often hear the declaration and new revelations, they have discovered such a rhema word in so many different other areas of ministry for the saints, but they seem to have willfully failed to ascertain a rhema word on sexuality. Rhema (ῥῆμ in Greek) means an "utterance" or "thing said." It is a word that signifies the action of utterance. In Christianity, it is used in reference to the concept of Rhematos Christou, Jesus Christ's sayings.

> Looking unto Jesus the author and finisher of our faith; who for the joy that was set before him endured the cross, despising the shame, and is set down at the right hand of the throne of God. For consider him that endured such contradiction of sinners against himself, lest ye be wearied and faint in your minds.
> *Hebrews 12:2-3*

I was troubled when I was being raised because I did not ever recall specifically studying the subject matter of homosexuality in our family Bible study sessions. However, I heard my dad preach about being delivered from the spirit of homosexuality. In addition, my mother expressed her disdain for gays and the Gay Rights Movement and its negative effects on this country. She supported the sentiments of the Evangelicals in their stance about the progression of the gay community. It is their opinion that the wickedness of Gay Rights is the reason why the United States is on its way to hell in a hand basket. Their attitudes are shared without reservation among many Christians. I am not completely sure if my parents still embrace their anti-gay principles, but I know beyond a shadow of a doubt they have evolved. At least three of my six siblings voiced their viewpoints regarding their anti-gay standpoints more so than the opposition of my parents. My other siblings have displayed their unchanging love for me. Their love for me has never changed, even though at the age of 40 I shared my truth with them concerning my spirituality and sexuality, in a short self-published book entitled *Son of a Bishop, My Testimony*.

I experienced emotional turmoil and I heard strong convictions coming from my family members who I love and adore. Two of my siblings, who are the most non-religious of the bunch, have always displayed very low tolerance for religious hypocrisy. They both warmed my heart in the most loving way, with kind words from my oldest sister Angelia, who expressed her love for me on a phone call before reading my book. She told me she did not care what the book contained and wanted me to know she loved me. Moreover, I received a beautiful message of support in a letter from my youngest brother, Christopher, who informed me he read my book and he was very proud of me. My eyes welled with tears, as I was very touched by his words because I was his big brother.

I remember as a child sitting in one of my dad's revival church services. He was preaching about being delivered from the strongholds of the devil and having the determination to stay delivered. He gave an example of a young man in Little Rock who was the church's organist. My dad was in Arkansas conducting revival church services, holding a prayer line for people who wanted to be delivered from various evil spirits.

He told us about this particular young man who was effeminate and stepped into the prayer line for deliverance. My dad said that he prayed without ceasing for this young man and finally an evil spirit was cast out of him. The young man straightened up and started to strut in a very masculine manner and started talking with bass in his voice and testified, "Thank God for delivering me, I am a man, I am a man!" My dad and the congregation rejoiced.

My dad said he returned to Little Rock the next year and asked that same young man if he was holding on to his testimony. My dad said the young man responded in a very soft and effeminate manner, "Yes, I am." I wonder if he lost his faith or was he just being his authentic self.

A person experiences deliverance when he or she is freed or delivered from being possessed by a demon or evil spirit.

> "...the idea of one's sexuality can only with great violence be divorced or distanced from the idea of the self."—
>
> *-James Baldwin*

four

Stop The Madness!

"You were not born with homosexual desires."
"Homosexuality is an evil spirit or a generational
curse that has a stronghold over you."
"You must be delivered. Only the Holy Ghost will be able to set you free."
"Homosexuality is unnatural and it is not a part of God's holy nature."
"You chose to be that way."
The above statements are some of the strong sentiments inflicted upon the
souls of many in and outside of traditional religious places of worship.

Preachers passionately and arrogantly disseminate these kinds of messages and others that one must be set free and Holy Ghost delivered from the evil of homosexuality, which is not God's best choice.

The religious establishment propagates this popular statement:

"The Bible is certain that we are all born into sin and you must be born again."

Yes, that holds true for everyone. They disingenuously place an undue and unjust burden on people who were born innately with same gender attraction.

People who use the mantra "hate the sin, love the sinner" as it refers to innate sexuality condemn a cross-section of people in the name of religion. They are being oppressive in a prejudiced system of institutionalized hate and intolerance that is certain to boost more religious bigotry. Their behavior does not glorify God nor Christendom.

I believe it outrageous and disingenuous when people compare adults coming together for love or lust to the act of murder, bestiality, or any other egregious act. Many Christian churches seem to subscribe to the mission of convincing those who are attracted to the same sex that something went wrong early in their life. That posture may be noble if some kind of sexual abuse warranted that kind of counsel; however, it must be very wise counsel with wise solutions. Most same sex oriented people were never sexually abused. I must point out the fact that I have never been a victim of sexual molestation and I have never molested or sexually abused anyone.

Unfortunately, most victims of sexual abuse were taken advantage of by trusted neighbors, friends, family members, or respected leaders in the community. I become infuriated when an adult decides to involve himself or herself sexually with a minor in order to fulfill his or her sick, selfish, and perverted desires. They have childhood issues that were never dealt with properly. They are perhaps replicating the same experience or something similar that probably happened to them as a child. Their madness has developed into a vicious cycle.

We tell children to stay in their place and adults should follow suit when it comes to sexual relations. I believe it is neither godly nor wise to persuade someone that their homosexuality exists due to being overtaken by an evil spirit or a generational curse. People can be burdened with the lifelong task of trying to free themselves and be Holy Ghost delivered from the evils of their innate sexuality, which leads to a maddening cycle of hypocrisy. Many people associate an individual's homosexuality with the ills and the vicissitudes of general wrongdoing, crimes, debauchery, and the transgressions of life, which are different subject matters.

"Are homosexual adults in general sexually attracted to children and are preadolescent children at greater risk of molestation from homosexual adults than from heterosexual adults? There is no reason to believe so. The research to date all points to there being no significant relationship between a homosexual lifestyle and child molestation. There appears to be practically no reportage of sexual molestation of girls by lesbian adults, and the adult male who sexually molests young boys is not likely to be homosexual. (Groth & Gary, 1982)

> "The vast majority of child molesters are male,
> and most sexual abusers were sexually abused as children."
> *(Goetz, 2014)*

five

> Discrimination is a hellhound that gnaws at Negroes in every waking moment of their lives to remind them that the lie of their inferiority is accepted as truth in the society dominating them.
> - *Martin Luther King, Jr.*

"If you are Practicing Homosexual, You Can't be a Christian"

I am disturbed when the relationships of same gender loving people are reduced to "disgusting sexual acts." Heterosexual or so-called straight people are not the only ones who can have a loving, monogamous, emotional, intimate, nurturing and long-term relationships. These covenants are not exclusive to them by any stretch of the imagination.

Fundamentalists have created a prejudicial religion that fuels a discriminating judgment and mandate for the homosexual man and woman. Their condescending statement, as is the title of this chapter, emanates from that poisonous ideal that has been injected in divisive doctrine, which is a deep-seated problem with Fundamentalist Christians in the Body of Christ (organized Christendom). The title of this chapter is certainly not true, scriptural or godly. There is nothing sinful about being heterosexual or homosexual. A person chooses sin, not their sexuality. The Fundamentalist Christian establishment has been riding roughshod over same gender loving Christians long enough.

I strongly believe and trust in the sovereign God of all creation who has established one of His laws of nature in me. I am fearfully and wonderfully made by Him. His works are marvelous. I strongly believe in the sovereign God of all creation because of this very reason – He is sovereign. God does exactly what He wants to do without considering the ideology of our thoughts and feelings of how we think that he should operate and rule all of his creation.

> I will praise thee; for I am fearfully and wonderfully made:
> *Psalm 139:14*

Anyone can make a prejudiced statement that is popular among traditional religious church folk. However, if a person applies the rightly divided word of God to his or her life and understands it within its proper context, then that person can establish truth, and not follow the popular religious traditions of men.

> Study to shew thyself approved unto God, a workman that needeth not to be ashamed, rightly dividing the word of truth.
> *2 Timothy 2:15*

I have learned to love and embrace God's word even when some religious practices have demonized His word and even when I do not understand the great mysteries of His sovereignty.

I believe the purpose of homosexuals and same gender love is identical to that of heterosexuals and their love. Many heterosexuals procreate and some do not; some homosexuals procreate and many do not. God fulfills Himself in all humans and nature.

> For as many of you as have been baptized into Christ have put on Christ.
> 28 There is neither Jew nor Greek, there is neither bond nor free, there is neither male nor female: for ye are all one in Christ Jesus.
> *Galatians 3:27*

> For God so loved the world, that he gave his only begotten Son, that whosoever believeth in him should not perish, but have everlasting life.
>
> *John 3:16*

We undermine the valuable, innovative, and powerful contributions of our former civil rights leaders and the forefathers of this country when we use divisive double standards to uphold prejudice and bigotry in the name of religion. To put your foot on the necks of a people that you fail to understand is the epitome of the "crabs in a bucket syndrome."

> "Power at its best is love implementing the demands of justice. Justice at its best is love correcting everything that stands against love."
>
> *- Martin Luther King, Jr.*

An oppressor is someone or something, be it a system or organization that harshly dominates or subjects a person or a people to a harsh or cruel form of domination.

A bigot is basically an intolerant person who refuses to accept different views.

I can cite many examples of personal, domestic and government wielded oppression that subjects people to harsh and cruel treatment. We are now seeing the results of institutionalized oppression unraveling worldwide. For instance, people in several Middle Eastern nations are amid unrest oppression by dictators and tyrants for generations. They are now fighting relentlessly for their freedom and their oppressors are losing their strongholds.

Even the U.S. experienced problems with oppression. The United States is a fairly young nation, built upon the promises of equality for all people. It is the land of the free and the home of the brave and where everyone has the right to live their life with liberty and pursue happiness. However, U.S. history as it relates to oppression is quite embarrassing based on the initial pretense of its development. Some of its citizens have faced oppression and the evils of slavery, the oppression and discrimination that ultimately motivated the Women's Rights Movement, the Civil Rights Movement, and Gay Rights Movement. We are fortunate that the oppressor has completely lost regarding slavery and is losing regarding the rest of the oppressive ills in our society today. However, we still see shades of oppressive behavior surrounding sexuality and it is still very acceptable and evident in many of our religious institutions.

The oppressors are everyday people like you and I who participate in forming systems and upholding those systematic institutions, religions and even attitudes that judge, discriminate, and repress people. Those individuals are bigots, and they operate in the name of religion.

six

Who Told You That You Were Naked?

I am reminded of a sermon by a friend of mine, Tommie L. Watkins, Ph.D. In his book entitled *Living Out Loud*, Rev. Tommie, as I refer to him, made a very interesting and profound revelation. He referenced this particular Biblical story with the *New Revised Standard Version (NRSV)* Bible about the fall of mankind in:

> "So God created humankind in his image, in the image of God he created them; male and female he created them (1:27). And the man and his wife were both naked and were not ashamed (2:25). They heard the sound of the Lord God walking in the garden at the time of the evening breeze, and the man and his wife hid themselves from the presence of the Lord God among the trees of the garden. But the Lord God called to the man and said to him, Where are you? He said, 'I heard the sound of you in the garden, and I was afraid, because I was naked; and I hid myself. He said, 'Who told you that you were naked?'
> *Genesis 1:27, 2:25, 3:8-11a (NRSV Bible)*

Rev. Tommie made the following points: He was made just like Adam and Eve, uniquely and authentically by the Divine Creator to be and to live a healthy life. He, too, just like Adam and Eve, allowed the words and opinions of others to become gods, superior to the word of God. Also, he allowed people and circumstances to convince him he was naked as he tried to hide in the trees of unhealthy pretentious relationships and friendships, self-righteousness and alcoholism because he was so afraid to be who God created him to be: totally exposed, naked, true, open, and feeling no shame, never realizing that "playing the game" and manipulation was not required of him.

My take away from that sermon, other than the beautiful points already made by Reverend Tommie, is:

> There is no fear in love. But perfect love drives out fear, because fear has to do with punishment. The one who fears is not made perfect in love.
> *1st John 4:18 KJV*

My understanding of sexuality is that sex and erotic emotions are a by-product, or a manifestation of, spiritual and mental emotions. The natural process of having sex and erotic feelings for another person should be tempered with the proper understanding of love, lust, marriage, monogamy, sex education, and the blessing of mature spiritual counsel, which promotes self-worth. If you don't surround yourself with tender love and care, your erotic and sexual emotions can sometimes lead to unhealthy sexual escapades and liaisons that sometimes develop into a sexually decadent way of life. You will eventually suck the life and joy out of your body and soul. Some of our youth have found themselves in deplorable situations because they have been overtaken by adult sexual predators who have victimized them and caused great physical and mental harm.

seven

Holy Rollers

When I was age 14, my family attended revival services at a row house located on 6th Street in Harrisburg, Pennsylvania. The house, which was converted into a makeshift church, was named, At The Cross Church of God In Christ. However, my family members and I were members of Lingo Memorial C.O.G.I.C, which was located a few blocks away on Division Street in the uptown section of the city. Harrisburg, like most urban cities in the Northeast, was crammed with a plethora of two and three-story historic colonial styled row houses. My family's house, located on Liberty Street in the Allison Hill section of the city, was no different.

The temperatures were freezing one Friday night with several inches of snow on the ground, but that little house-church was quite warm, and filled with the saints singing, dancing and sweating to the glory of God. I made a conscious decision that night to accept Jesus Christ into my heart and into my life, I became "saved" and to particularly "seek God for the Holy Ghost" although the Bible tells us that it is a gift from God known as the spirit of truth and the comforter. I was faced with a major decision, especially for a boy with six siblings who all had varying and intertwining senses of humor about church folk and image and culture that surrounded the holiness church.

I expected jeers from a couple of my brothers and sisters when I was awash with emotions of praise and worship during the church service. I stood and clapped my hands to rhythmic sounds and beats of the piano, drums, organs, and tambourines with tears flowing from my eyes. Then I would break out into a full-fledged holy dance shuffle with my arms tucked like I was doing the funky chicken. My siblings burst into a roaring laughter, but I didn't care. No one really knew what I was experiencing. I really needed God to deliver on his promise as stated in the books of John and Psalm.

> For the LORD God is a sun and shield: the LORD will give grace and glory: no good thing will he withhold from them that walk uprightly. John 14:13 And whatsoever ye shall ask in my name, that will I do, that the Father may be glorified in the Son
> *Psalm 84:11*

I did not rest on the laurels of my parents' prayers; I was going for broke by living a consecrated sanctified life. I was battling and fighting against serious thoughts and feelings concerning my sexuality. I did everything I knew to be right and holy. There were many years praying, appealing, petitioning and even demanding that God free me of this "evil." I wondered why God was withholding this good request from being granted. Mom was a missionary and church mother and my father was an evangelist and auxiliary bishop. They were, and still are to this day, what I deem spiritual veterans in the C.O.G.I.C. community. I knew my life and soul was at stake.

C.O.G.I.C. and other Holiness/Pentecostal styled churches had a custom of what was called tarry services. Tarry is defined as to remain or to wait in expectation of somebody or something. I tarried for the first time for the Holy Ghost. I repeated the name of Jesus so many times while being coached by seasoned adult saints who yelled in my ear. They chanted, "Call him! Call his name!" I became tongue-tied and started to foam and spit from the mouth. One of the ladies yelled in my ear, "That's it!"

The Pentecostal/Holiness church folk use the term purging for foaming or spitting from the mouth while tarrying for the Holy Ghost. One definition of purge is to remove something or being cleansed. After I experienced that somewhat stressful and yet hopeful traditional religious experience of purging and calling on the name of Jesus, I literally felt cleansed and changed. I felt God had rid me of this serious unnatural issue that was swirling around inside of my mind. However, I never felt my thoughts unnatural. My religion and culture prodded me to believe it was not godly or natural for a God-fearing person to have natural, spiritual, mental, and physical emotions for the same gender.

I believe homosexuality carries such a stigma and a reproach in traditional Christian homes, churches, and the community at large. Many men and women will and have gone to great lengths to distort the truth about their own realities. Anytime you seek the approval of people who do not understand your reality and you allow their opinions to manipulate you into misrepresenting your own life, you are susceptible to develop self- hatred and self-destruction. It will set in and your whole life can become a lie, you will not totally love yourself, and it could destroy you.

eight

"...the idea of one's sexuality can only with great violence
be divorced or distanced from the idea of the self."—
–James Baldwin

WHY ME?

One of my sisters attended and eventually joined a church on Allison Hill when she was old enough to make her own decisions about where she wanted to worship. Although the number of church congregants was relatively small, the church was attended by a large number young adults and children. They were very excited about the pastor because he was concerned about their souls. The Pentecostal-Holiness style church vibrated from the pulsating sounds of the band. The lead and bass guitarists who jibed in-sync with a pianist, a drummer, and mixed with the Holy Ghost, the congregation sang and danced in the spirit with great fervor. My oldest brother, Anthony, was one of the very brilliant guitarists in the band. In church speak, they were "on fire for the Lord." For some reason, my sister was drawn to this congregation. The women were told not to wear pants. However, she was accustomed to that because our parents banned pants, make-up, and jewelry in our household. The women in the church could not expose their elbows and toes. They wore little white-laced tapestries atop their head as a covering. I attended this church with my sister for approximately a year.

At age 17, I enjoyed worshipping God at this church with so many other young people. The pastor was very charismatic, clever, and just a comical individual who really knew and understood people. He made me laugh. I thought he was very wise. He had the ability to charm you in one breath, and in another breath he would prophesy, rebuke, and scare the hell out of you. I recall on this particular Friday night, he asked two men who were visiting the church to come to the front of the church during what was called "Open Rebuke Session." He told them God told him they were homosexuals. I and the audience gasped. I figured I was next, but he did not bother me.

He had made a similar declaration during another service. He asked each young adult to stand up and he declared God told him that they had lustful spirits. The only two individuals he did not call out were his future son-in-law and I. I just knew that this would be the moment of truth and that I would be exposed of this homosexual spirit that was nagging at me.

I would oftentimes get into the special prayer lines during revival services and hope God would reveal my secret to the evangelist or the preacher. I hoped that perhaps they would cast that devil out of me. I could not figure it out and no one could explain why I was given this type of cross to bear. I was never molested by anyone. I did not have any homosexual influences from any of my relatives or friends. I had a great relationship with my mother and my father. As a matter of fact, they both declared I was a blessed child and God would someday use me.

I have never participated in, nor have I ever had any proclivity for pedophilia, bestiality, gang rape, or orgies. This is also true for most same gender loving people I know. I had, and have, resisted, fasted, prayed and cried out to God for my deliverance and it has not yet come even after having faith that one day it, this thorn in my flesh, will go away.

So, is it that the straight man or woman is blessed above others? Are they privileged only to deal with the natural temptations of the flesh after being born in the same world of sin? Are gay people doubly cursed for not having natural affection and attraction towards the opposite sex and for the affection and attraction for the same sex? Has God played a dirty trick on homosexual people? Does God really care about the gender of whom we love and have affection and attraction for? Why has he not delivered me? I often ask myself these questions.

Many Christians, and those who oppose homosexuality, assign molestation, outside influences, a dysfunctional family, or other maladies of life as reasons for one's "chosen" homosexuality. I attempt to display how these kind of intimidating, dogmatic practices and tactics from the traditional church can damage one's psyche.

nine

Deliverance, Truth or Choice

Leaders of Christian organizations feverishly admonish people who are possessed with or rumored to have that so-called homosexual demon/spirit to resist it for it will flee. They instruct homosexuals to never to give in to it while they wait on the Lord to deliver them. They say, "God will deliver you and set you free." It becomes their lifelong task to trust God for their complete deliverance after they have passed their many tests of same-sex temptations. They attest God will eventually free the homosexual of that sickness and brokenness. They propagate that unnatural evil emotion never leaves you, but just keep on holding on because He is able to do anything, Amen!

Deliverance is defined in religious circles as the process of freeing someone who is possessed by a demon or an evil spirit. Contrary to the popular belief of Christians, I believe it is a very dangerous and an unloving practice to use the Bible to lead a young man or woman to live a life of concerted deception based on traditional religion and personal ideology. Concerted deception is when a person decides to make personal choices contrary to their God-given innate sexuality in order to please family and church society. Traditional religion and personal ideology has led many in our places of worship toward mental and spiritual anguish as they try to change something that God never asked anyone to change. Some church folk have inflicted some of the most subversive, anti-Christ behaviors on many of God's same gender loving children. They are responsible for hurting and damaging many of these souls.

The churched homosexual is forced by anti-homosexual proponents to claim he or she is spiritually free and fake spiritual deliverance from himself or herself. I believe God is not a weakling. I know this to be true based on what he does and who he is. He does all things well and he does not make mistakes. I see his magnificent creations around the world. To suggest that a person's sexual identity is a choice, or is a struggle of the human will battling against God, is an insult to Jesus the Son of the sovereign God of this universe.

I will pose the following questions and share my personal choices as an example.

Do you remember the day and the exact time you decided to become attracted to a male or female?

Do you remember how you thought to yourself that you would try a woman today and then try a man tomorrow?

If you think about that for a few minutes, you will realize these are a couple of pretty ridiculous questions. If you feel you actually had a choice in choosing what gender you genuinely have intimate, romantic, spiritual, and sexual attraction for, then I am afraid you are probably lying to yourself and the person with whom you are or have been intimate. When you choose to wear green contact lenses instead of brown ones, this is clearly a choice.

I chose not to lie anymore to myself, my family, and friends and the women with whom I have been intimate in my life. I chose not to live by the beat of my ego and my masculine pride to marry a woman as a facade to satisfy my perceived image problem.

I choose to understand that sexuality is not nearly all about a sexual act. I choose to hold on to my faith in God and to allow Jesus the Christ to be the Lord of my life when most in Christianity reject my authenticity. I choose to study and understand the Holy King James version of the Bible within its proper context in order to reject the anti-gay religious tradition, which is truly anti-Christ. I choose to understand the divisive and prejudiced anti-gay sentiments in Christianity, certainly not created by the loving and sovereign God, but created by flawed people within Christianity.

I choose to understand the covenant of a union of love between two people. God was established well before the legally binding state contract of U.S. marriage, which is a civil right for all people. Ultimately, I choose and try to live my life authentically and unapologetically with integrity. I have made these real choices.

ten

Authenticity

In May 2013, Jason Collins, a 34-year-old National Basketball Association player, became the first active athlete in major American sports to come out of the closet and proclaim that he is gay. He will go down in history for his act of courage, but not without some negative controversial statements from ESPN Analyst Chris Broussard. Broussard basically stuck a pin in Jason Collin's bubble of good energy and the congratulatory tidings that poured in from fellow athletes, celebrities, U.S. President Barack Obama, and other politicians. Chris Broussard's critique of Jason Collins was that he is a sinner for proclaiming his truth and Broussard feels justified in his judgment due to the fact that he is a Christian.

Broussard's comments and those of others who condemn gays, homosexuality, and same gender love by identifying it as sinful are nothing more than an institutionalized prejudiced religious myth.

Broussard wrote that his belief lies in his religious background. His religious background is the problem! On the contrary, his religious background has very little to do with the Gospel of Jesus Christ, but rather the prejudice that dominates the subject matter of homosexuality. Jesus Christ suffered enough on the cross. So why should anyone place more suffering by inflicting pain to people in his name?

Jesus was all about truth and he was not into the religious traditions of men and their judgments and inconsistencies. Jesus Christ – the epicenter of Christianity – never said a negative word concerning same gender love. The word "homosexuality" was added to newer versions of the Bible in the 1940s.

Collins underwent a lot of soul-searching and self-evaluating to understand and embrace his truth after many years of lying to himself, family and society. It is a very big deal for anyone to finally come into their truth and find peace within them and with God. He should be celebrated for displaying great courage and fortitude.

It is my understanding that the common denominator of most religions and their purposes for an individual is to walk in truth, honesty, peace and integrity. However, most Christians don't celebrate people who become honest and authentic about their sexuality in order to live in their God-given truth.

In February 2014, Michael Sams, a 21-year-old National Football League potential draftee decided to share his truth with the world concerning his sexuality. He too stated he is gay. Sams made his decision of integrity before the NFL Draft, which is the selection process that determines if a college football player will play professional football. After Sams was drafted, he become the first openly gay NFL player. His truth and integrity is a key factor that should be celebrated by religious leaders and organizations. If the fundamental religious leaders demonize his truth and integrity, I wonder what else is left for our youth to stand on.

My heart breaks that it has become business as usual, and judgment and condemnation as usual at every hand when we hear or read about another person who has found peace with God concerning their sexuality. We should meet them where they are in a vein of self-actualization and truth. We have a chance to proclaim and reinforce the good news of the gospel of Jesus Christ by cheering them on to live a life of integrity and prudence and avoiding the pitfalls of promiscuity.

I am a son of ministers, and a son of the church. I am a product of this religious tradition. I am a Christian man who truly loves God and I too came into my truth as a gay man with my family a little bit later in life than Jason Collins and by far later in my life than Michael Sams.

I am speaking from the perspective of a man who could have easily married a woman and I could have taken the traditional family route. I could have entered into the ministry in the traditional church and perhaps comfortably lived a life on the so-called "down low" in order to appear as a pillar in my church, family, and community.

It took me 40 years to become true to myself and embrace my God-given, innate authenticity. I am by far more liberated and spiritually fulfilled than living a conflicted mangled mess of a life involving other innocent people in order to please the expectations of family, friends, and church folk. I did not want to live my life as a facade or in a distinguished disguise, which would have nothing to do with pleasing God or loving myself.

I read many books related to homosexuality, including *What the Bible Really Says About Homosexuality*, by Daniel Helminiak, Ph.D. Bishop Eddie Long's book, *Gladiator, Strength of a Man*, transforms men into gladiators who stand against injustice amidst impossible odds.

After I read those books, I secured a more solidified viewpoint. I have grown spiritually in the most non-traditional manner, and I truly know my purpose. I am ready to help eradicate the prejudice and the ignorance that surrounds sexuality, which prevents people from completely loving and embracing one another around the world. A real man loves God and his family. He has integrity, takes care of his responsibilities, and protects the least among us.

I have a monogamous covenant partner, Derrick Tinsley, Sr., of several years, and we share a very special love for each other. We have a sacred bond of praying and worshipping God together. We both know and realize our spiritual bond keeps us away from the pitfalls and temptations of life.

My partner and I first met at a mutual friend's home during a house warming party. We instantly bonded as we stepped away from everyone else and held an engrossed conversation about our beliefs, relationships, and our mutual religious backgrounds. Our conversation was deep, but at the same time we laughed about the commonalities of the traditional holiness style type of worship experience and the seriousness surrounding spirituality and sexuality.

Derrick and I eventually knew and realized both of us were at the crossroads of our individual futures. Our very special connection transcended Derrick's diabetic/health issues. Derrick accepted my new mission and assignment to write and sometimes vocalize this subject in a public manner. We were both very much the "Don't Ask – Don't Tell" type of guys and very comfortable with living that way in our individual lives. That has changed and I know this is my ordained task.

We share a home where my heart and soul is happy I feel it is my covenant duty to love, be true, protect and take care of my partner just as I take care of myself. We have the blessings of God our father and that's the only approval we need.

Chris Broussard said that gays and those who live in unrepentant sin are walking in open rebellion to God and Jesus Christ. My focal point, the Bible, does not define same gender love as sinful. Church folk use scripture to condemn homosexuality, gay people, and same gender love, but their plea has absolutely nothing to do with love. The King James Version Bible scripture in Leviticus 20:13 addresses bisexuality for the Israelites. The story of Sodom and Gomorrah in Genesis 19 condemns gang rape with a parallel story in Judges Chapter 19.

Romans 1 addressees a group of people who turned from God to worship idol sex gods and then participated in orgies and other immoralities. 1 Corinthians 6:9 condemns male prostitution and their customers. However, the Gospel does not condemn same gender love or marriage equality. When people feel forced to live in a closet of hypocrisy, they subject themselves to the breeding ground of a life filled with dishonesty, a double life, and the creation of scandals.

eleven

Context is the Key

I truly believe some leaders of today's Christian religion should repent for the unloving rebellion against gay people and same gender love, which is not a person's choice. They should repent for misrepresenting God's love and his sovereignty.

I would really love to see more Christians mature and examine the Bible. It should be understood within its proper context executing the spirit of its wonderful virtues. We must veer away from the teachings of some of our former teachers of Christian faith who ignorantly and divisively misunderstand the subject matter of homosexuality.

It is Jesus who is the author and finisher of our faith as believers or Christians. It is a well-known fact that Jesus who is the reason of why we exist as Christians never condemned same gender love or homosexual covenants.

Opponents of same gender love base their rationale and justify their disdain on the writing of the apostle Paul. He was one of the strongest teachers and preachers of the Christian faith. However, we must deal with his writings within the proper context of when, why, and for whom the verses were intended.

The gay person bears a heavy burden when various verses of scriptures have been used out of context for generations. The scriptures are used outside of their original context to denounce a gay person's spiritual, emotional and natural need for companionship.

A few stories in the Bible address immoral incidents that some leaders in the Christian faith refuse to address within the context of origin. Some Christians have made concerted efforts to highlight certain verses that are used to corrupt the church world for generations, demonizing the orientation of gay, homosexual, or same gender loving people. Same gender love and innate sexuality are completely ignored and are egregiously tied to immorality and the stereotypes of a particular act of sex, which has nothing to do with love and companionship.

The Apostle Paul addressed an infamous group of people – saints in Rome. Many Christians use this particular chapter – a letter or epistle - to justify their convictions to define homosexuality as sinful. They handpicked specific verses and to this day even some Christians cherry-pick verses to isolate and sensationalize the sexual acts to cast an image of rampant orgies and idol worship. In the story, these heterosexuals had whole-heartedly and purposefully turned their backs on God and changed their sexuality to participate in lust-filled orgies. Men were having sex with men and women with women to worship idol gods of animals and sex.

Consequently, God abandoned these people and left them to their own devices because they callously left him.

My father, a well-studied and traveled seminary trained evangelist and preacher and a former auxiliary Bishop within the C.O.G.I.C. organization, confirmed this incident and judgment in Romans 1, which addresses a specific sect of people. Their indictment was predicated on the following verse:

> And changed the glory of the incorruptible God into an image made like corruptible man, birds, four-footed beasts and creeping thing.
> *Romans 1:23*

This verse has nothing to do with me, a man who loves and serves the Lord. I admonish you to read the Romans 1 within its proper context without cherry-picking specific verses. This chapter was a letter and an address to a sector of believers in Rome. Paul warned and rebuked those who turned their backs on God. And he stated very clearly in verse 7 who he was addressing:

> To all that be in Rome, beloved of God, called to be saints:
> Grace to you and peace from God our Father, and the Lord Jesus Christ.
> *Romans 1:7*

twelve

And Such Were Some Of You:

I cannot recall any example in the Bible where Jesus or his disciples performed a miracle of changing, healing, or converting someone's sexuality from gay to straight.

The question and man's divisive argument of defining homosexuality as sinful or as a choice would not exist if that was the case.

Some people point to 1 Corinthians 6:11 as proof that one's sexuality can be changed. It follows a list of behaviors in verses 10-1, which are wrongdoings, crimes, debauchery and the transgressions of life that will prevent you from inheriting the Kingdom of God.

> Know ye not that the unrighteous shall not inherit the kingdom of God?
> Be not deceived: neither fornicators, nor idolaters, nor adulterers,
> nor effeminate, nor abusers of themselves with mankind, Nor thieves,
> nor covetous, nor drunkards, nor revilers, nor extortioners,
> shall inherit the kingdom of God.
> *1 Corinthians 6:9-10*

> And such were some of you: but ye are washed, but ye are sanctified, but ye
> are justified in the name of the Lord Jesus, and by the Spirit of our God.
> *1 Corinthians 6:11*

Those who condemn homosexuality rely on 1 Corinthians 6:9 to condemn homosexuality and attempt to send gay people to hell. They have replaced the words in that verse "effeminate" and "abusers of themselves with mankind" with words or phrases such as homosexuals, sodomites, and men who sleep with men. The Greek word for effeminate is "malakoi," which is defined as a male prostitute and the Greek word for "abusers of themselves with mankind" is "arsenokoites," which is an obscure Greek word that some Greek scholars refer to as the customer or the dominating figure of the male prostitute in Roman culture of that day. There are numerous mistranslations of that word in the numerous translations of the Bible. Strong's Exhaustive Concordance of the Bible:

733 arsenokoítēs (from 730 /árrhēn, "a male" and 2845 /koítē, "a mat, bed")

As for arsenokoitai, some scholars believe Paul was coining a name to refer to the customers of "the effeminate call boys." We might call them

"dirty old men." Others translate the word as "sodomites," [•sodomites: Hebrew word "Kadesh, a quasi sacred person," a male devotee by prostitution to licentious idolatry; - sodomite, unclean.]

For instance, the 1611 King James Bible version avoids a direct translation of the word "homosexual" with the phrase "abusers of themselves with mankind." However, it is interesting to note that even though the word homosexual did not exist at the time and wasn't even coined until the late 19th century. In 1611, a word did exist, which if used by the King James translators, would have left no question as to what they were referring to. This word is "invert," which meant "homosexual," but they did not use that word. (Ellis, 2104)

Church folk tend to confuse and associate an individual's same gender attraction with general bad behavior, wrongdoing, crimes, debauchery, and the transgressions of life. Many people have repented and made up their minds to change their bad behavior with the guidance of scripture and prayer. They are a far cry different from the façade of a person who wears green contact lenses over their brown eyes in order to deceive or fit into the majority of a green-eyed society. That person would still remain brown-eyed at the end of the day. Christians demonize gay people as being evil and that our basic needs for spiritual, mental and physical intimacy and companionship is an abomination and completely off-limits for covenants and marriage. When a person is inflicted with such restrictions and pain in God's name, that person suffers spiritually and mentally. We would witness a travesty and a miscarriage of justice for the soul of that man or a woman.

thirteen

> Marriage is honourable in ALL, and the bed undefiled:
> but whoremongers and adulterers God will judge.
> *Hebrews 13:4 KJV*

Marriage Equality Is Honorable for All People

In May 2012, President Barack Obama took a strong position in support of same-sex marriage.

Some religious leaders are unfair, unjust, and ungodly, to give an authoritative order to God-fearing people who are born naturally with spiritual, mental and physical emotions for the same gender. They are unfair to declare that gay people are to live out their days on earth and never marry or have a monogamous covenant with a spouse in order to please the Lord and their religious affiliations. I am not referring to having sex with multiple partners and living a decadent and devious life of orgies, prostitution, pedophilia, rape, adultery and sexual promiscuity, which are sexual sins that are condemned in the Bible. However, many people do attribute these sins to homosexuality. They could be no further from the truth for me and most gay, same gender loving homosexuals I know and love.

I would be completely disingenuous if I did not acknowledge that some of the aforementioned behaviors are very prevalent in the gay and straight communities as well. Gays do not have a monopoly on this kind of behavior by any stretch of the imagination.

I do not believe a person should marry a heterosexual/straight person and ignore their natural, spiritual, mental and physical emotions for the same gender in hopes that God will change their desire.

If God does not change a person's desire, then that person's life will be filled with lies and deceit. God is able to do anything and He knows what he is doing. We sometimes do not trust that He does. God is sovereign. Furthermore I don't recall an example in the Bible where God or Jesus miraculously changed someone's sexuality from gay to straight or from homosexual to heterosexual.

The religious community seems to circumvent biblical truth in order to interpret scripture completely outside of historical context. They alter scripture displayed in the many other versions of the Bible to uphold man-made religious customs that can destroy a person's soul. If you compare the King James Version Bible text to other bible versions NIV, NKV, and others, and specifically look at the verses traditionally used against homosexual people, you will discover bias and audacious prejudice operating in some of the newer Bible versions. When you add a word or take away a word from a sentence or a paragraph, you can change the entire meaning or direction of its original intent.

As Christians, we should be followers of Jesus the Christ. We are to live by the example and the instructions he has laid out for us in the New Covenant of the New Testament. We should allow the loving spirit of his words to abide in our hearts in order to become living testaments for the world. Although we have the New Covenant of Jesus, some Christians still enjoy perusing verses from the old law in a judgmental manner in order to condemn others when they know they are not living by the old Law of Moses.

I believe the Bible is like a road map for our lives. The Old Testament displays the conditions of that road before Christ came and fulfilled the Law of Moses, which demonstrated the history of that map's rough mountainous wilderness roads of trees, brush, and gullies. After Christ came and fulfilled the Mosaic Law, he created a New Covenant. That old wilderness-road map was updated with new interstates showing us how to get to the same destination without the difficulty of that old Wilderness Road.

Even though Jesus, who is the son of God, fulfilled the law through his life, death, burial, and resurrection, he extracted key points of the law that were included in the New Testament, which is the New Covenant. However, some Christians still prefer to travel down that miserable old wilderness road of tradition and veering way off course and outside of context in order to berate and condemn others. They discount the sacrifice of Jesus dying on the cross at Calvary.

Here is an example of what the King James Bible actually states:

> "If a man ALSO lie with mankind,
> as he lieth with a woman,
> both of them have committed an abomination."
> *KJV - Leviticus 20:13*

Here is an example of what New International Version states:

> "If a man has sexual relations with a man as one does with a woman, both of them have done what is detestable. They are to be put to death; their blood will be on their own heads."
> *NIV Leviticus 20:13*

The word "also" means in addition. So that verse and Chapter 18:22 seems to address bisexuality or an orgy of sorts instead of the verse explicitly reading, "A man shall not lie with mankind." The King James Version example has been tainted by the New International Version to infer something to the contrary.

My agenda is to proclaim the truth of the Bible and the gospel of Jesus Christ, which is for all people. Jesus already suffered for us on the cross at Calvary. So no one, especially the children of God, should place more suffering on a population of God's misunderstood children – gay people. Many Christians seemingly do not care to understand this situation because they continually inflict pain in his holy name.

I do not think mainstream church congregations have a problem with taking responsibility for the creation of the popular environments of intolerance surrounding sexuality and marriage equality. They take a firm stance and believe it is their religious duty to stand against this "unrighteous sin."

I do not see where it says homosexuals or same gender love will be judged. Sin takes place when a heterosexual or a homosexual takes part in adultery, whore-mongering, killing, stealing, lying, anger, idol worship, or to knowingly do wrong.

I believe the covenant of love between two individuals constitutes a union. A wedding ceremony is a formality and a state marriage license grants a couple state and federal benefits, which are legal rights. So, when the Christian leaders quote scripture outside of its original context and intent to support their personal prejudice and profess it comes from God, we must realize that God has nothing to do with that. God is sovereign.

Christian fundamentalist organizations have built bedrock of philosophy on the demonization of homosexuality and what constitutes a marriage. Unfortunately, the traditional African-American church and the African-American community, which I identify with, has become the most common predator to those who have been marginalized in our society. Blacks have been maligned in the name of the God that I serve through Jesus.

We have seen this nagging pattern repeat itself, and the victim usually ends up becoming the predator in the worse way. We can recall a dark time in US history – the slavery of blacks and the unjust Jim Crow South that was justified by some Christians who misused and abused scripture to uphold their passionate slavery ideology. African slaves and African-Americans were the victims during those particular times in history.

Same gender loving people have hearts and souls just as heterosexual people. We are a very diverse people and we exist in every nationality, religion, country, and community. We vary from conservative to liberal, celibate to promiscuous, masculine to effeminate, spiritual to the heathen, just as heterosexual people. We do not fit into one or two stereotypes and we all are not part of the same lifestyle. Sexuality is not a lifestyle.

fourteen

Was Jesus Aware of Gay Folk?

When Jesus was teaching about marriage and divorce, he granted very limited reasons for divorce between a man and woman in Matthew 19:3-12 KJV. He taught about an obscure group of people called eunuchs. The scripture reads as follows:

> 3The Pharisees also came unto him, tempting him, and saying unto him, Is it lawful for a man to put away his wife for every cause?
> 4And he answered and said unto them, Have ye not read, that he which made them at the beginning made them male and female,
> 5And said, For this cause shall a man leave father and mother, and shall cleave to his wife: and they twain shall be one flesh?
> 6Wherefore they are no more twain, but one flesh. What therefore God hath joined together, let not man put asunder.
> 7They say unto him, Why did Moses then command to give a writing of divorcement, and to put her away?
> 8He saith unto them, Moses because of the hardness of your hearts suffered you to put away your wives: but from the beginning it was not so.
> 9And I say unto you, Whosoever shall put away his wife, except it be for fornication, and shall marry another, committeth adultery: and whoso marrieth her which is put away doth commit adultery.
> 10His disciples say unto him, If the case of the man be so with his wife, it is not good to marry.

> 11But he said unto them, All men cannot receive
> this saying, save they to whom it is given.
> 12 For there are some eunuchs, which were so born from their mother's womb: and there are some eunuchs, which were made eunuchs of men: and there be eunuchs, which have made themselves eunuchs for the kingdom of heaven's sake. He that is able to receive it, let him receive it.
>
> *Matthew 19:3-12 KJV*

In my attempt to support by position, I came across some information during my research of this subject. Rick Brentlinger, a profound teacher of faith, wrote a Web-based article entitled, "The Testimony of Jesus - Our Lord." Brentlinger's work can be found at www.gaychristian101.com. He wrote as follows:

1. Eunuchs so born from their mother's womb. These eunuchs, according to Jesus, were born that way. They did not make a personal choice to be eunuchs and they were not physically castrated by men. Some Christians believe these men were homosexual eunuchs.

2. Eunuchs made so by men via physical castration. These eunuchs were physically castrated and could not consummate marriage.

3. Eunuchs who made a personal choice to be eunuchs, by abstaining from marriage, for the kingdom of heaven.

Jesus distinguishes the third class of eunuchs, who made a choice to be eunuchs, from the first class, who did not make a choice to be eunuchs. According to Jesus, born eunuchs are exempt from the Adam and Eve style, heterosexual marriage paradigm. The common traditionalist tendency is to read into that exemption that all eunuchs must therefore be celibate, an assertion Jesus never makes.

fifteen

What are Eunuchs?

Eunuchs are mentioned throughout the Old and New Testaments, but the Bible does not provide us much information on what defines a eunuch other than their occupations, duties, and assignments. Faris Malik has completed a thorough, exhaustive study on eunuchs.

Since 1991, Malik has been researching the subject of eunuchs and ancient conceptions of sex and gender identity. He states the innately and exclusively homosexual men of the ancient world inhabited the category of eunuchs. He said: "What we moderns think of as a eunuch, namely a castrated man, was simply an artificially manufactured homosexual. Natural and man-made eunuchs co-existed as distinct categories for at least a thousand years, from the first-reported mass castrations about 600 BCE until 400 CE. The willingness to engage in homosexual activity – particularly intergenerational – was widespread among men in the ancient Mediterranean region. Women and boys were considered equally tempting sex objects for those whom we would call heterosexual men. However, the ancients did differentiate based on an unwillingness or incapacity for heterosexual sex. Certain men were known to fundamentally lack arousal for sex with women, and men of this kind were distinguished from the majority of ordinary men on that basis. The innately and exclusively homosexual men of the ancient world inhabited the category of eunuchs. What we moderns think of as a eunuch, namely a castrated man, was simply an artificially manufactured homosexual.

You can obtain more information about this elaborate study/thesis produced and written by Faris Malik at www.well.com/user/aquarius/thesis.htm

Although Jesus was very specific about the limited reasons for divorce in the previous chapter, people deem divorce is acceptable and practiced on a regular basis within the church world outside of the realm of what Jesus actually excused.

Other biblical scripture seems very clear about the silent role of women in the church and their duty to be subservient to men.

> Let the woman learn in silence with all subjection. But I suffer not a woman to teach, nor to usurp authority over the man, but to be in silence.
> *1 Timothy 2:11-12*

Contrary to this scripture, women have been appointed to church leadership roles and the numbers are at an all-time high.

Homosexuals are bombarded with about five or six Bible verses used by Christians that are completely outside of its original context with an intent to demonize the homosexual. They face acceptable anti-gay prejudice, which is at an all-time high within many of our places of worship.

When any church's agenda becomes so judgmental, mean spirited and practices alienating and demonizing people by inflicting pain in God's name, we face a humanity problem that literally could be considered religious bullying. I believe something is fundamentally wrong.

Jesus, Apostle Paul, and the eunuchs of the Bible will confirm for you there is no mandate or commandment to marry the opposite sex and procreate.

> "To be fully seen by somebody, then, and be loved anyhow- this is a human offering that can border on miraculous."
> *– Elizabeth Gilbert*

sixteen

Church Culture Can Be a Breeding Ground for Hypocrisy

We live in a culture where it appears more important to keep up with the Jones's and the Trumps. Many people feel the need to be perceived as successful. They believe it is very crucial to their image and self-worth.

The perfect image of family in the eyes of our friends and church members seem to hold more value than love, truth, and humility until we see the examples and hear the stories of the crap hitting the fan or the truth taking its time to catch up.

We have religious leaders who are living double lives as pastor, loving husband & father at the same time this man is filled with unrest during his spare time surfing the internet, combing the alleys and city streets for male companionship.

The intuition of a particular pastor's wife had always existed because she sensed her husband's affection for men before they married. However, she made a conscious decision to never talk about it in hopes God would miraculously change him since he is a "man of God," or that she would be able to do it.

Meanwhile, she is faced with the dilemma of keeping the powerful family image intact or risk damaging the facade everyone enjoys. I wonder why they would live such a complicated life.

It is yet customary for Evangelical, Baptist, and Pentecostal Holiness church folk to hammer the anti-homosexual tradition with scripture from the pulpit. Their ritual and tradition has castigated so many souls to submission and others to their own destructive devices.

The people who are sincere and faint at heart would tend to exist in a judgmental atmosphere of self-hate and torture. It breeds an environment of hypocrisy for the devious ones who refuse to stand for truth and those who just go along with the program.

I was born and raised in one of the largest and most extreme anti-gay religious organizations. C.O.G.I.C., which has always had a large number of closeted members, including deacons, missionaries, church mothers, ministers, elders, pastors, and bishops, who fight and rally against their own sexuality. They gladly fall in line with the traditional anti-gay theology, which births ultimate hypocrisy on a very large scale.

Many more years of my life were spent in a very large congregation as a longtime member of a now infamous bishop in the Atlanta, GA area. He was notorious for his bashing and slashing of the many gay members in his congregation with cutting and insulting sermons for many years.

For some reason, I believe he had a greater revelation of truth on the subject matter of homosexuality. He preached some sermons that resonated within me during some of his most intimate and transparent sermons that gave me a sense he was on his way of becoming bold enough to declare contextual scriptural truth regarding sexuality. He boldly proclaimed truth and broke tradition in many other areas of traditional religion in his congregation.

I really thought the transparency he seemed to display at times would supersede him and catapult his ministry to a level beyond the traditional prejudiced anti-gay religious community. I felt this bishop's sincerity in his desire to see his congregants excel spiritually and naturally. I loved the fact that he was a very charitable leader and for the most part, he did not play the money gimmick games of fleecing his members with the reward of special prayer lines to compensate them for their participation in special money offertory collections.

I was sadly disappointed about the well-known accusations of same-sex encounters and the manipulation of several young men in the congregation that came against this bishop. I was much more disappointed when this bishop failed to rise to the occasion of accountability after settling in the court of law with his accusers.

Many people would be able to rely on the truth and keep their integrity when faced with public adversity and stay dutiful to a higher calling. After being indoctrinated around hypocrisy for most of my life, it has been struggle to fully unmask the truth even as I share with you as I write. If my dirty laundry was aired so publicly, would I be able to stand in the court of public opinion? Would you?

As a believer of Jesus Christ who grants forgiveness to others, I grapple with losing trust and respect for a spiritual leader. Although I left this congregation shortly after the scandal, I have close friends and associates who were quite troubled that I faithfully attended this bishop's church for so many years in spite of the many notorious brutal homophobic type sermons. However, I believe the bishop's anti-gay sermons were lightweight compared to those that emanated from my C.O.G.I.C. roots.

I continue to speak of the good will this bishop shared with his parishioners and followers worldwide. He reinforced my former teachings of studying God's word for myself and allowing me to become spiritually independent, relying on God, and God alone. I've fallen in love with Jesus over and over again for his sacrifice and what he is to me and what he actually represents to the world through the teachings of this bishop.

seventeen

My Contention & Observation on HIV/AIDS in Our Communities of Color

Some so-called religious people claim HIV/AIDS is a judgment from God against homosexuality.

The African Americans, as well as people of other cultures, are very much entrenched in religion that demonizes homosexuality. Even people who do not attend church services and those who possess very little biblical knowledge on the subject matter profess a very pronounced judgment against homosexuality. I would say their prejudice against homosexuality has reached an epidemic level and has a stronghold in our communities. Their judgmental behaviors perpetuate prejudice, hypocritical religious closeted gays, self-loathing, and homophobic character, which negatively influence our society.

Personally, I don't believe that HIV and AIDS is a judgment from God against homosexuality because if it is a judgment, we would not witness the harsh judgment on many innocent heterosexual women of color, or poor nations. This epidemic should be a wake-up call to the Christians, to be shaken awake from a daze of organized judgment and open rebuke aimed at the gay community. Christians should take this titanic-like disease that is affecting many innocent people by the helm in a loving Christ-like manner. They should accept the lives of gay people and closeted individuals with the true love and the gospel of Jesus, which is non-discriminating and non-alienating.

Jesus Christ's teachings are not anti-homosexual. Christians should proclaim that we are fearfully and wonderfully made by the all-knowing and loving creator, and that he did not make a mistake when he created a homosexual or heterosexual. Christians should promote self acceptance, monogamy, and marriage for homosexuals. I believe that would be key to halting the spread of HIV/AIDS and other diseases.

> Marriage is honourable in ALL, and the bed undefiled:
> but whoremongers and adulterers God will judge.
> *Hebrews 13:4*

Unfortunately, most Christians have decided to amplify their microphones that blare anti-homosexual prejudice in the name of God. They call out homosexuality sin as an abomination based on their flawed interpretation of scripture. They have taken the liberty to rewrite the Bible to fit their logic and ideology. I believe this is very dangerous.

Homosexuals may be different from the status-quo, but Christians have a responsibility to embrace homosexuals as they do anyone else and minister the Gospel of Jesus Christ. They should not inflict anti-homosexual religious tradition.

I believe this HIV/AIDS matter in our communities of color is simply about throwing caution to the wind. Many gays choose to have unprotected sex and in many cases not face the real truth and brutal honesty about their sexuality, which stems from generational and traditional religious homophobic rhetoric. Some preachers use their pulpits to condemn homosexuality as sin and that can force some people to forsake the truth of who they really are. They resort to live in the closet and participate in much of the so-called down low or DL promiscuous sexual activity in our communities, which spreads disease. Our beautiful women of color and the souls of many other men and women are victims of this crime committed by stubborn religious traditionalists who demonize one's innate sexual identity as an abomination.

My goal and my endowment from God is to encourage all people to study, live, and learn the life of Jesus Christ and to steer clear of the religious traditionalists who pervert the true Gospel of Jesus with their own discriminating ideologies.

Same gender loving couples should be taught the same Christian principles regarding relationships and marriage in our traditional places of worship as are heterosexual couples. They should be encouraged to put God first and foremost, pray together, love and value yourself, and love and value your mate. Harming one another mentally, physically and sexually should not be tolerated, nor accepted. If Christians preached those same principles instead of the judgment and rebuke, homosexuals would feel loved by God and the community and not feel forsaken by God as the traditionalists have preached. There would be less down low sexual promiscuity and more spiritual responsibility. There would be much less disease. There would be more love.

eighteen

Jesus is Not Your Scapegoat for Bigotry

A definition of scapegoat is a person made to bear the blame for others. This word originated from a religious tradition in the Old Testament of the Bible. Goats were used in the ritual of Yom Kippur noted in Leviticus 16. The Israelites' sins were symbolically attached to the goat and that animal was sent into the wilderness to be destroyed.

I implore Christians to stop using Jesus and identification as a Christian to discriminate and support personal prejudice and bigotry concerning homosexuality. Jesus has already suffered for the sins for all of mankind. Christians should stop inflicting pain on others in Jesus's name.

Church doctrine, divisions, traditions, denominations and religious ideology only voice man's religious preferences and personal prejudices. Again, the original passages have been altered to read differently in other versions of the Bible only to discriminate.

God is sovereign, and He does not operate and design people according to religious tradition.

The truth of God's word understood in its proper context will always confirm itself.

Truth always arrives a little later than the speedy popular lies and customary deceptions that people tend to cling to and engage themselves in. But once old truth arrives, it cannot be stopped or reversed. We can reflect back in history to colonial U. S. slavery to see that. We can point to many Bible verses to justify slavery, if the verses are taken outside of the context in which they were written.

I charge you as Christians and people of God to be guided by the truth of God's love.

Please lay down the dogma and prejudiced traditions of man's religion and live by the light of his love.

Conservative Christians should never be about the divisive business of fighting against any organization or an individual for so-called Christian Rights. They should follow the example of Jesus and the divine love he displayed while on Earth. And, moreover, a Christian heart is the only inspiration one should aspire to display.

I do not think people should identify themselves as a liberal or a conservative because we are individuals with vacillating opinions about life. I believe Jesus was both a conservative and a liberal. He was very traditional in his passion about people and telling the truth. He was very concerned about the matters of our hearts and souls, and our faith in Him. He was very generous with his love for us even to His death on the cross at Calvary. He was also very liberal in standing for justice for the sick and poor. He also stood against the religious traditions and hypocrisy of the scribes and Pharisees who were the religious leaders of that day.

I love the Lord God with all of my heart. He has given me a peace that surpasses all of the misunderstandings of the deep seated traditional religious prejudices of men. They have absolutely nothing in common with the Gospel of Jesus.

I just don't believe that the Bible should be used as a divisive tool to demonize a population of God's creation whom in most cases were born naturally with spiritual, mental, and physical emotions for the same gender.

> "I was against gay marriage until I realized I didn't have to get one."
>
> *-James Carville*

nineteen

Evelyn & Dennis Schave, Evidence of an Olive Branch

In the spring of 2010, just when I was thoroughly convinced that most of the living pioneers and the so-called Saints of Old were all stuck in a time capsule, possessed by the tradition of men without illumination and no new revelation of the word of God when it came to the truth about homosexuality, I ran across the article "The Testimony of Evelyn Schave."

In the C.O.G.I.C., we call the older holy ghost-filled, Bible-grounded men and women "seasoned saints." We describe them as being cut from the cloth of the Saints of Old. As I read Evelyn Schave's testimony, my soul was touched and lifted because I was totally convinced she was definitely the truth from the old school of tradition. She said, "I was raised in the old conservative, Pentecostal, 'everything's a sin' movement."

After reading sister Evelyn's testimony, I wanted and needed more. I sent her an email and we began to correspond. She forwarded a copy of her wonderful book that chronicles her transition in ministry from so-called Old Time Religion to restudying the word of God on the subject matter of homosexuality.

Her book is entitled, *For Such a Time as This*. A few weeks later, Sister Evelyn, as I refer to her, communicated in an email that she and her husband would be in Atlanta for a three-day revival service. I replied that I would make it my business for my partner and I to attend Pastor Randy Morgan's New Covenant Church of Atlanta that Sunday morning.

Sister Evelyn possesses a very sweet disposition, like my mother, and Brother Dennis Schave, her husband, like my father, has a very kind and confident spirit. They are one of the most humble and sweetest couples I have ever met. They are anointed and packed with the power of love and truth.

Sister Evelyn ministered the unadulterated word of God in her traditional old school fashion, yet she reached out to those men and women who were broken, backslidden, and cast out of their traditional churches due to their homosexuality.

I had never before witnessed such and electrifying church service. My eyes continuously flowed with tears. She preached a message of restoration and inclusion to former ministers of the gospel. She identified stragglers as those who have fallen behind due to feeling unwanted and unworthy to take their rightful place in church service, what many refer to as the body of Christ. Sister Evelyn and Brother Dennis began to embrace and pray with the people individually as some fell to their knees, weeping in the spirit of contrition. The church was filled with the love and comforting Spirit of God.

The living and deceased Seasoned Saints, including people of my parent's and the Schave's generation, set the tone and put into motion the movement that interprets scripture to condemn homosexuality in today's society. I am so very grateful that Sister Evelyn and Brother Dennis allowed God to lead them into their life-changing restudying of His Word. I sincerely pray that others will do the same.

You can live a life of hell, bitterness, and promiscuity as a heterosexual or homosexual or you can live a Christ-centered life as a heterosexual or homosexual and bear the fruits of the spirit.

> But the fruit of the spirit is love, joy, peace, long-suffering, gentleness, goodness, faith 23 meekness, temperance: against such there is no law.
> *Galatians 5:22*

twenty

> "Above all, don't lie to yourself.
> The man who lies to himself and listens to his own lie comes to
> a point that he cannot distinguish the truth within him,
> or around him, and so loses all respect for himself and for others.
> And having no respect he ceases to love."
> - *Fyodor Dostoyesky*

Reconciliation

There are several ministers of the Gospel in the Atlanta area who have stepped out on faith to proclaim the good news or Gospel of Jesus while reconciling their spirituality with the truth of their own sexuality.

My heart is filled with joy when I visit Bishop O.C. Allen's Vision Church of Atlanta, Pastor Dennis Meredith's Tabernacle Baptist Church in Atlanta, Pastor Randy Morgan's New Covenant Church of Atlanta, Bishop Jim Swilley's Church in the Now and Dr. Kenneth Samuel's Victory for the World Church in Stone Mountain.

A few other pastors I know in the Atlanta area provide a refuge of inclusion to the traditionally renounced individual. Each of these pastors speaks with love, compassion, and the conviction of the Holy Spirit to the many souls that pack pews in their sanctuaries weekly.

I am puzzled when I listen to most of Christendom's key megachurch pastors and televangelists like Bishop Eddie L. Long, Bishop T.D. Jakes, Pastor Joel Osteen, Pastor Rick Warren and Bishop Charles E. Blake Sr. They are very eloquent in their delivery. They are influential, charismatic, intelligent and seminary-trained. I believe they fully understand the differences of teaching and preaching from the holy-scriptures within the context of the chapters and verses of the Bible.

If I use church-speak, these pastors would be called experts in "rightly dividing the word" of God. I wonder if they would rather preach and proclaim scriptural truth or take comfort in those religious traditions that have been ingrained into the brain of church society. I believe the whole truth of the Gospel of Jesus Christ should be considered greater than the fear of breaking flawed religious customs, traditions and doctrines.

twenty one

Uganda! Uganda! Uganda!

Members of the Uganda Parliament passed a horrible bill that persecutes and demonizes people they simply care not to understand. They are marginalizing their innate God-given sexuality as sinful when the Bible says no such thing. Their actions mirror the religious scribes and the Pharisees of the Bible, which Jesus judged harshly for their own hypocrisy. They were overly concerned about outward appearance of man's religious traditions and their rules and regulations. Some Ugandans seem to be only concerned about the dead letter of the law withholding and denying the spirit of truth from the soul of men.

> For all the law is fulfilled in one word, even in this;
> Thou shalt LOVE thy neighbour as thyself.
> *Galatians 5:14*

  This is the most powerful and necessary of all passages in the Bible that defines a person's spiritual walk with Christ other than truly believing Jesus is the Son of God.
  We would have an entirely better world if we all loved our neighbors as we love ourselves in this godly manner:

> 22 But the fruit of the Spirit is love, joy, peace,
> longsuffering, gentleness, goodness, faith,

> 23 Meekness, temperance: against such there is no law.
> 24 And they that are Christ's have crucified the
> flesh with the affections and lusts.
> 25 If we live in the Spirit, let us also walk in the Spirit.
> 26 Let us not be desirous of vain glory, provoking
> one another, envying one another.
> *Galatians 5:22-26 KVJ*

These are truly the qualities of a holy and moral person.

Love is defined in the dictionary as a profoundly tender, passionate affection for another person. The dictionary goes on to state that love is a feeling of warm personal attachment or deep affection, as for a parent, child, or friend.

When a person believes Jesus is the Son of God and the commandment to love one another, that belief supersedes the 66 books of the Bible and trumps the Mosaic-Levitical law. The Israelites abided by that law before the coming of Jesus. Some very religious people refuse to accept that the so-called "Law of Moses" served its purpose for those people in history. Some people have boldly gone against scripture to preserve parts of that Law of Moses by distinguishing ceremonial and moral laws, which have no scriptural basis in separating the two.

Jesus gave instructions in the New Testament of the Bible, and his instructions are very sufficient for living a moral and holy life.

twenty two

More Evidence of an Olive Branch

I will provide the following example of what will unfold when true Christians lay down divisive doctrine and their religious tradition that have harmed and posed an obstacle of derision for a misunderstood population of people for many generations. My soul leaps and my heart stays filled with hope for Christendom when I think about what happened a few years ago in the heartland of America. I pray for a ripple effect from the center of our country to each coast and then across this globe.

In June 2011, Rev. Eric Elnes, Pastor of Countryside Community Church, Omaha, Nebraska, and area ministers publicly unveiled a proclamation calling for an end to religious and civil discrimination based on sexual orientation. Rev. Elnes said the proclamation was created because, "we were just fed up with the popular notion that the Christian point of view is anti-gay."

The Heartland Proclamation
By the Heartland Clergy for Inclusion As Christian clergy

We proclaim the Good News concerning Lesbian, Gay, Bisexual and Transgender (LGBT) persons and publicly apologize where we have been silent. As disciples of Jesus, who assures us that the truth sets us free, we recognize that the debate is over. The verdict is in. Homosexuality is not a sickness, not a choice, and not a sin. We find no rational biblical or theological basis to condemn or deny the rights of any person based on sexual orientation. Silence by many has allowed political and religious rhetoric to monopolize public perception, creating the impression that there is only one Christian perspective on this issue. Yet we recognize and celebrate that we are far from alone, as Christians, in affirming that LGBT persons are distinctive, holy, and precious gifts to all who struggle to become the family of God.

In repentance and obedience to the Holy Spirit, we stand in solidarity as those who are committed to work and pray for full acceptance and inclusion of LGBT persons in our churches and in our world. We lament that LGBT persons are condemned and excluded by individuals and institutions, political and religious, who claim to be speaking the truth of Christian teaching. This leads directly and indirectly to intolerance, discrimination, suffering, and even death. The Holy Spirit compels us:

to affirm that the essence of Christian life is not focused on sexual orientation, but how one lives by grace in relationship with God, with compassion toward humanity;

to embrace the full inclusion of our LGBT brothers and sisters in all areas of church life, including leadership;

to declare that the violence must stop. Christ's love moves us to work for the healing of wounded souls who are victims of abuse often propagated in the name of Christ;

to celebrate the prophetic witness of all people who have refused to let the voice of intolerance and violence speak for Christianity, especially LGBT persons, who have met hatred with love;

Therefore we call for an end to all religious and civil discrimination against any person based on sexual orientation and gender identity and expression. All laws must include and protect the freedoms, rights, and equal legal standing of all persons, in and outside the church.

> We're here for a reason. I believe a bit of the reason is to throw little torches out to lead people through the dark.
> – Whoopi Goldberg

twenty three

Thank You President Obama!

I was not initially a staunch Barack Obama supporter during the 2008 Democratic presidential campaign. I really didn't know much about you. As a matter of fact, I was enthusiastic about Senator Hillary Clinton because I liked her. I felt she was the better candidate with more proven experience and she had the "Bill Clinton Momentum" behind her. I would have been pleased with a President Hillary Rodham Clinton.

During the party's campaign to select its nominee for president, I came to know you by watching your speeches and debates on TV. Also, I got chance to read your background and history from various news sources and skimming through a couple of your books.

I was struck by what you stood for. I would always tell my friends I loved that you always appeared to be honest, and have integrity with the working class, the poor and the maligned. I saw you as a compassionate man with a big heart.

Some of my friends were not happy that I continued to support Senator Hillary Clinton during the primaries, but I would always tell them that if you were to win the primaries that you would have my full support. Ever since your victory as the Democratic nominee and election as president, you have had my unyielding support.

I have never been a flighty person or one to give in to peer pressure and to change my mind due to popularity. I feel that loyalty and personal conviction is very important in every aspect of one's life. I have always believed that consistency and the aforementioned qualities are some keys to success, which is what I have seen from you during the primaries and during your first term as the President of the United States of America, and now your second term. Congratulations! My prayers are with you.

I thank you for standing up for same gender loving covenants. Your decision to do so has become a voice of reason for some in the traditional religious community to stretch beyond their personal and religious doctrine of prejudices of sorts. There are many examples in the Bible of where Jesus had to admonish some of the religious leaders and some of their traditions of that day.

I thank you, First Lady Michelle Obama, for being the president's loving wife and partner. You have enhanced his core values of equality that you both share. I thank you Sasha and Malia, for being the inspiration and motivation of your father's sense of fairness for all people and for future generations.

President Obama, I believe that you exemplify real Christian values and I believe that you live by this quote:

> "Before you speak to me about your religion, first show it to me in how you treat other people. Before you tell me how much you love your God, show me how much you love all of His children; Before you preach to me of your passion for your faith, teach me about it through your compassion for your neighbors. In the end, I'm not as interested in what you have to tell or sell as in how you choose to live and give."
>
> *~Cory Booker, Newark, New Jersey*

twenty four

My Conclusion

I conclude that there is a clear disconnect between the reality of sexuality versus traditional religious dogma that identifies and defines homosexuality as sinful. You will almost never hear or participate in a bantering discussion justifying lying, cheating, stealing, and adultery in most topic of conversation.

I finally started asking God for his will to be done in my life. It is not about my sexuality or who I may have or may not have as a companion. My main concern is am I being true to God and true to who he has created me to be. I strive to allow his love and truth to flow within me in order to shine outside as light to others in hopes it will lead them to accept God's love. And I pray that his love will flow within them so that they too will become a light of love.

We should be thankful and respect God for his magnificent creative energy and power that has designed each person's life to be completely different from that of another. We should respect the differences in one another.

We undermine all the teachings of goodness, love, peace, truth, holiness and community when we isolate and deny another community of God's sovereignty. Christians should not identify by popular prejudiced Christian traditions, but only the organic Gospel of Jesus.

God knows what he is doing, but most traditional religious folk don't seem to trust that he does. It took me a long time to fully surrender to God and to have peace about not being like everyone else and knowing that I could be used by him just as I am. I am a man with a surrendered heart, soul, and mind.

I tried to deceive myself and others about my God-given sexuality in order to fit into the religious society and the society of the moral majority until God helped me see he didn't make a mistake among the millions of people who are same gender loving, gay, lesbian, bisexual, transgendered, inter-sexed, and homosexual. I believe He desires for us all to worship Him in Spirit and in Truth. God reminded me that His yoke is easy and his burden is light.

> For you created my inmost being; you knit me together in my mother's womb. 14 I praise you because I am fearfully and wonderfully made; your works are wonderful, I know that full well.
> *Psalm 139:13*

> So The Last Shall be First, and the First Last;
> for many be called, but few chosen
> ***Matthew 20:16***

Epilogue

The purpose of this epilogue is to document the progress of marriage equality in the United States of America since the initial publishing of this book.

On June 26, 2015, The U.S. Supreme Court ruled that states must allow same sex marriage, which is a landmark victory for marriage equality.

Some religious organizations will comply and have already welcomed and embraced this new law of the land in their places of worship. Many institutions of traditional religion have immediately rejected and doubled down on their anti-gay stance and rhetoric in spite of the following verses of Scripture that speak to obeying the laws of the land in a version of the Bible that has been embraced by many.

Romans 13 New International Version (NIV)

Submission to Governing Authorities

13 Let everyone be subject to the governing authorities, for there is no authority except that which God has established. The authorities that exist have been established by God. ² Consequently, whoever rebels against the authority is rebelling against what God has instituted, and those who do so will bring judgment on themselves. ³ For rulers hold no terror for those who do right, but for those who do wrong. Do you want to be free from fear of the one in authority? Then do what is right and you will be commended. ⁴ For the one in authority is God's servant for your good. But if you do wrong, be afraid, for rulers do not bear the sword for no reason. They are God's servants, agents of wrath to bring punishment on the wrongdoer. ⁵ Therefore, it is necessary to submit to the authorities, not only because of possible punishment but also as a matter of conscience.

⁶ This is also why you pay taxes, for the authorities are God's servants, who give their full time to governing. ⁷ Give to everyone what you owe them: If you owe taxes, pay taxes; if revenue, then revenue; if respect, then respect; if honor, then honor.

Works Cited

"American Standard Version." *Wikipedia*. Wikimedia Foundation, 25 Feb. 2014. Web. 13 Mar. 2014. <http://en.wikipedia.org/wiki/American_Standard_Version>.

Brentlinger, Rick. "FREE Online Bible Classes." *Gay Christian 101*. N.p., n.d. Web. 13 Mar. 2014. <http://www.gaychristian101.com/>.

Brown, Samuel M. "Son of a Bishop, My Testimony." *Http://sonofabishop.blogspot.com*. Rosedog Publishing, May-June 2006. Web. <http://www.amazon.com/Son-Bishop-Samuel-Marcus-Brown/dp/0805988106>.

Chris Connelly | Outside The Lines. "Mizzou's Michael Sam Says He's gay." *ESPN*. ESPN Internet Ventures, 10 Feb. 2014. Web. 12 Mar. 2014. <http://espn.go.com/espn/otl/story/_/id/10429030/michael-sam-missouri-tigers-says-gay>.

"CHRISTIAN KKK." *Www.kkk.com/*. N.p., n.d. Web. <http://en.wikipedia.org/wiki/Ku_Klux_Klanwebsite by entering its URL or by searching for it.>.

Cunningham, Rev. Jim. *Gay Christian Survivors*. N.p., n.d. Web. 13 Mar. 2014. <http://gaychristiansurvivors.com/>.

"Duck Dynasty Controversy." N.p., n.d. Web. <http://www.aetv.com/duck-dynastyite>.

Ellis, Rev. Bob. "Mercy To All. NET." *Mercy To All. NET*. N.p., n.d. Web. 13 Mar. 2014. <http://mercytoall.net/>.

Elnes, Rev. Eric. "Heartland Proclamation." *Heartland Proclamation The Proclamation Comments*. N.p., n.d. Web. 14 Mar. 2014. <http://www.heartlandproclamation.org/>.

"ESPN's Chris Broussard Calls Homosexuality a Sin During Jason Collins Segment (Video)." *The Hollywood Reporter.* N.p., Apr.-May 2013. Web. 13 Mar. 2014. <http://www.hollywoodreporter.com/news/espns-chris-broussard-calls-homosexuality-448377>.

Fisher, Michael. "The Ku Klux Klan The Ku Klux Klan Is Composed Entirely of White, Anglo-saxon, Christian American Citizens, Both Male a." *The Ku Klux Klan The Ku Klux Klan Is Composed Entirely of White, Anglo-saxon, Christian American Citizens, Both Male a.* N.p., n.d. Web. 30 Mar. 2014. <http://home.wlu.edu/~lubint/touchstone/KKK-Fisher.htm>.

Goetz, Bracha. "Things You Need to Know About Child Molesters." - *Abuse.* N.p., n.d. Web. 12 Apr. 2014. <http://m.chabad.org/theJewishWoman/article_cdo/aid/1707466/jewish/Things-You-Need-to-Know-About-Child-Molesters.htm>.

Groth, Dr. A Nicholas. "Facts About Homosexuality and Child Molestation." *Facts About Homosexuality and Child Molestation.* N.p., n.d. Web. 11 Apr. 2014. <http://psychology.ucdavis.edu/faculty_sites/rainbow/html/facts_molestation.html>.

Helminiak, Daniel, Ph.D. "What the Bible Really Says about Homosexuality." N.p., n.d. Web. <http://www.visionsofdaniel.net/book3WBRS>.

The Holy Bible: King James Version ; a Word-for-word Reprint of the First Edition of the Authorized Version, Presented in Roman Letters for Easy Reading and Comparison with Subsequent Editions. Nashville: Thomas Nelson, 1990. Print.

King James Bible. S.l.: Stl, 1920. Print.

Long, Bishop Eddie L. "Gladiator Strength of A Man." N.p., n.d. Web. 13 Mar. 2014. <http://www.amazon.com/Gladiator-The-Strength-Long-Eddie/dp/1586029010>.

Malik, Faris. "Thesis: Eunuchs Are Gay Men." N.p., n.d. Web. 14 Mar. 2014. <http://www.well.com/user/aquarius/thesis.htm>.

Moo, Douglas. "New International Version Bible." *Wikipedia.* Wikimedia Foundation, n.d. Web. 12 Mar. 2014.

Pietrzyk, Mark E. "Homosexuality and Child Sexual Abuse." *Homosexuality and Child Sexual Abuse.* N.p., n.d. Web. 12 Apr.

2014. <http://www.internationalorder.org/scandal_response.html>.

Schave, Evelyn. "Schave Ministries - The Schaves." *Schave Ministries - The Schaves.* N.p., n.d. Web. 13 Mar. 2014. <http://www.schaveministries.org/The-Schaves.html>.

Strong, James. *Strong's Exhaustive Concordance of the Bible: Showing Every Word of the English Revised Version and the Authorized, or King James Version and Every Occurrence of Each Word in Regular Order ; Together with Dictionaries of the Original Hebrew Old Testament and the Greek New Testament.* Nashville: Broadman, 1979. Print.

"Theopedia, an Encyclopedia of Biblical Christianity." *Theopedia, an Encyclopedia of Biblical Christianity.* N.p., n.d. Web. 12 Mar. 2014. <http://www.theopedia.com/>.

Watkins, Tommie. "The Watkins Group, LLC - About Rev. Tommie Watkins Jr." *The Watkins Group, LLC - About Rev. Tommie Watkins Jr.* N.p., n.d. Web. 13 Mar. 2014. <http://www.twgllc.biz/pages/lol.html>.

White, Rev. Dr. Mel. "What The Bible Says and Doesnt Say About Homosexuality." N.p., n.d. Web. <http://soulforce.com/what-the-bible-says-and-doesnt-say-about-homosexuality-2/>.

Cover Art Design
By
William Bryant aka Bill-de-Barber
www.bill-de-barber.artistwebsites.com
tedeboi39@gmail.com

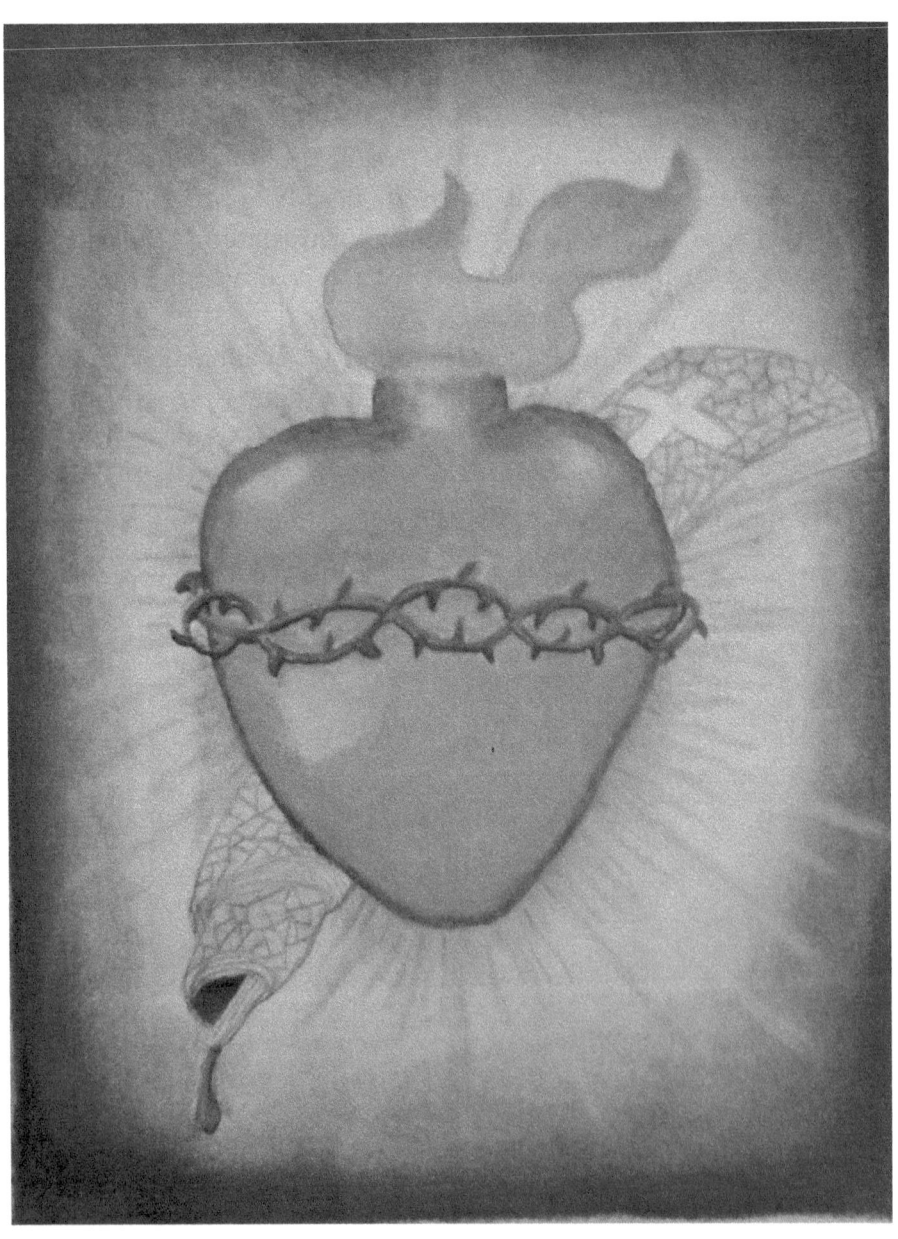

www.ingramcontent.com/pod-product-compliance
Lightning Source LLC
Chambersburg PA
CBHW071617040426
42452CB00009B/1374